PLAN, PANDEMONIUM

by Timothy Knapman
Illustrated by Miguel Diaz Rivas

OXFORD
UNIVERSITY PRESS

Chapter 1
The Great Pong

Marigold Mulch stood at the front of the school hall, holding up the Great Pong. Marigold was a plant expert. She was telling Lucy's class about all the weird and wonderful things she had found growing in faraway jungles.

Lucy was sitting at the front, listening with interest.

"The Great Pong is the most horrible-smelling plant in the world," Marigold explained. "If you ever got a good whiff of the Pong, your fingers would tingle and steam would come from your ears." She raised the glass case higher. "That's why I keep it in a glass case."

"Can't we have even a tiny sniff?" asked Bruno, Lucy's friend.

"Very well," said Marigold. She beckoned Bruno up on to the stage and lifted the case.

The moment the smell reached his nostrils, Bruno started wobbling. His face knotted, his knees knocked, and he fell over.

"Give him a second, and he'll be as good as new," said Marigold. "Now, before I go, I have a seed for each and every one of you."

From the floor, Bruno muttered, "I hope mine's a stinky one!"

Marigold rummaged in her deep pockets and handed each of the children a seed. There were big seeds and small seeds, stripy seeds and spotty seeds, jumping seeds and still seeds.

Lucy could hardly wait to find out what kind of seed she was going to get.

When it was Lucy's turn, however, Marigold said, "I'm terribly sorry, but I've run out of seeds."

Lucy was bitterly disappointed. She gave a big sigh.

Then Marigold said, "No, wait. I have just one more." She rummaged in her pocket again and brought it out. It was the strangest seed Lucy had ever seen. It looked like an egg. It felt like an egg.

"It's an egg," said Lucy.

"I am a famous plant expert," said Marigold, firmly. "Therefore, you can trust me to know the difference between a seed and an egg."

Marigold packed up to leave. "Good luck, children," she said. "These are super-fast-growing seeds, so when I come back in a week's time, they will all have grown into wonderful plants."

Marigold said, "Therefore, you can trust me to know the difference between a seed and an egg." Therefore means 'for this reason'. Can you repeat Marigold's line, starting with: *For this reason* … ?

Chapter 2
Seed or egg?

On their way back to the classroom, the children talked excitedly about their seeds.

"Quiet please," said their teacher, Miss Bliss. "Or you know what will happen …"

The children fell silent instantly. If ever they got too noisy, Miss Bliss would blow the battered, old bagpipes she kept in the classroom. They made the most dreadful squawk.

Miss Bliss and the teaching assistant, Mrs Anand, handed each child a flowerpot filled with soil.

Lucy looked at her seed again. The more she looked at it, the more she knew it must be an egg. "Miss ..." Lucy began.

"All right, everyone," said Miss Bliss, "you can plant your seeds!"

Lucy shrugged and popped her seed into the soil.

Of course, absolutely nothing happened. Lucy's seed didn't grow a single millimetre. All the other seeds grew super-fast, however.

The very next day, there were constant cries of "Yay!" as green shoots appeared in the other children's flowerpots. By the following afternoon, the classroom was full of flowers and plants.

What does 'constant' tell you about how often there were cries of "Yay!" the next day?

The other children kept saying, "Look how quickly my plant is growing!" and "Growing things is so easy."

"Humph," thought Lucy. "Perhaps I'm doing something wrong."

She went to the computer to <u>access</u> some information about making seeds grow, but all she found was – *Keep your flowerpot in a sunny place and water it* – and she'd already done that.

Lucy used the computer to <u>access</u> some information, which means she used it to find some information. When was the last time you <u>accessed</u> information on a computer, and what was it?

Chapter 3
Still not growing

The day before Marigold Mulch was due to return to the school, Miss Bliss asked, "Is your seed growing yet, Lucy?"

"No," said Lucy, "because it's not a seed. It's an egg."

"I'm sure Marigold wouldn't have made a mistake like that," said Miss Bliss. "I'm afraid your seed must have something wrong with it."

Lucy felt sorry for the seed or egg or whatever it was. Perhaps it was just shy. Perhaps that was why it was still hiding away in the flowerpot. It didn't mean there was anything wrong with it. She decided to take the flowerpot home with her that night to see if it would help. "Poor thing," Lucy thought, as she sat on the bus next to her mum.

Lucy tried some new ideas to get the seed to grow, including …

… taking the flowerpot on the trampoline and having a good old bounce,

… trying to feed it ketchup and ice cream,

… and telling it stories about famous plants from history.

When it was bedtime, Lucy kissed the flowerpot goodnight and said, "Whatever you are, I know you're wonderful. Please come out and say hello."

It didn't do any good, however. The next morning, there wasn't even the smallest bud poking up through the soil. Lucy sighed and took the flowerpot back to school.

All the other children were looking forward to showing Marigold Mulch their plants. Ubah had a rose, and Daisy had a daisy; Bruno had a stinkwort, and Grace had a fearsome crocodile-headed plant.

The children made their way to the hall.

"Can I stay here, Miss Bliss?" asked Lucy. After all, what did she have to show Marigold?

"Yes, if you really want to," replied Miss Bliss. "Start your homework while Mrs Anand gets the classroom ready for maths."

Lucy was soon bored. To cheer herself up, she started to whistle softly. That's when something odd happened. The flowerpot wobbled slightly.

Chapter 4
A big surprise

Lucy thought she might have imagined it, so she whistled again, a bit louder this time. There was no mistaking it … the flowerpot definitely wobbled! Now she whistled as loudly as she could. The flowerpot shook. Lucy gasped!

    She looked around for something that would make an even louder noise.

Of course! Miss Bliss's bagpipes! They were almost as big as Lucy, and picking them up felt like fighting a giant spider.

She took a deep breath and gave them a really good blow. Mrs Anand jumped in surprise and dropped the maths books.

At the very first screech, the soil in the flowerpot exploded. Lucy kept blowing and a stalk appeared. Only it didn't really look like a stalk. It looked like a leg. It had a flower <u>connected</u> to it that looked like a foot. Another stalk appeared and both stalk-legs waggled furiously.

There was a flower that looked like a foot <u>connected</u> to the stalk. Can you think of another word that you could use here instead of '<u>connected</u>'?

Lucy grabbed the flowerpot and turned it upside down so that the feet stood on the ground. The flowerpot cracked, and out burst a huge bird with a big snappy beak and small flappy wings.

"Bwark!" it said.

"Hello," replied Lucy.

"Argh!" screamed Mrs Anand, running out of the room.

Lucy tried to give the bird a welcoming hug, but it hopped out of her arms. Then it went for a <u>swift</u> trot around the classroom, gobbling up anything it could find.

"Please stop!" Lucy wailed, as she pulled a shredded maths book out of its greedy beak. The bird ate several chairs and an entire display about volcanoes, before Lucy finally managed to grab it.

> The bird went for a <u>swift</u> trot around the classroom. Does this mean that the bird went quickly or slowly around the classroom?

The bird wriggled in Lucy's arms as she carried it down the corridor, but she held on tight. Lucy couldn't wait to see the look on Miss Bliss's and Marigold's faces when they realized that she had been right all along.

When Lucy reached the hall …

… she got a big surprise.

She thought Miss Bliss would be proudly showing Marigold all the wonderful plants her class had grown. Instead, Miss Bliss was frantic. She was running around, screaming at the top of her lungs. This was because she was being chased by Grace's fearsome crocodile plant. It was hopping along the floor in its flowerpot.

chomp chomp

Can you name two things that Miss Bliss did that show she was frantic?

Chapter 5
Stop that plant!

Bruno told Lucy that as soon as they had got into the hall, the crocodile plant had jumped out of Grace's hands and had started snapping hungrily at the children.

"Don't you dare bite any of the children in my class," Miss Bliss had shouted. So the plant had decided to try to bite her instead.

The other children were hiding behind a pile of stacked-up lunch tables. Marigold, meanwhile, was chasing after the plant, carrying a big net.

"Just stay calm, Miss Bliss," she called out. "The plant is just responding to your fear."

At that very moment, Miss Bliss tripped over. The crocodile plant reared up with a <u>cruel</u> hiss.

The plant gave a <u>cruel</u> hiss. What else did the plant do that was <u>cruel</u>?

"Somebody do something!" cried Miss Bliss.

"Bwark!" said Lucy's bird. Everyone stopped and turned to look at it, and so did the crocodile plant.

"So it *was* an egg!" exclaimed Marigold. "I bought the super-fast-growing seeds from a market stall. Next door was a stall selling eggs. One of the eggs must have got mixed up with the seeds!"

Lucy might have said, "I told you so!" but, just then, her bird leapt from her arms crying, "Bwark!"

The fearsome crocodile plant took fright and bounced out of the hall and down the corridor.

"Stop that plant!" cried Marigold.

Bwark!

The crocodile plant was going very fast. There was no way Lucy's bird would be able to catch it before it escaped out of the school.

"In order to defeat the crocodile plant," thought Lucy, "I have to make my bird run faster … but how?" Then she remembered: "The bagpipes!"

As fast as she could, Lucy raced to the classroom and grabbed the bagpipes.

Lucy wanted to defeat the plant. How would you try to defeat a crocodile plant?

The whine of the bagpipes was all her bird needed. It put on a burst of speed and jumped on the plant before it reached the main door.

Marigold quickly put an upturned bin on top of the crocodile plant and sat on it, just to make sure it couldn't escape again.

"Hooray!" cheered Miss Bliss and the children.

brooom

Lucy took her bird home to live with her and her family, where it spent the rest of its days …

… having a good old bounce on the trampoline,

… eating ketchup and ice cream,

Bwark!

… and keeping an eye out for fearsome crocodile-headed plants.

Luckily, they never dared come near.

Read and discuss

Read and talk about the following questions.

Page 7: Can you finish this sentence? *Lucy's seed was really an egg, and therefore …*

Page 10: How do you think Lucy felt listening to the constant cries of "Yay!" from the other children? Would she have felt differently if there were fewer cries?

Page 11: Lucy uses a computer to access information about her plant. Can you think of another word or phrase that could be used instead of 'access'?

Page 20: Plants are usually connected to one spot. What was different about the crocodile plant?

Page 22: The bird moved swiftly. Can you think of another animal that moves swiftly?

Page 24: Why was Miss Bliss frantic? How might someone behave who was frantic?

Page 26: What does 'cruel hiss' tell you about what the crocodile plant was like?

Page 29: What did Lucy do to help her bird defeat the crocodile plant?